EXILES

POEMS BY

STEVE ELLIOTT

ISBN: 978-93-6354-654-7

First Edition: 2025
Rs. 200/-

Cyberwit.net
HIG 45 Kaushambi Kunj, Kalindipuram
Allahabad - 211011 (U.P.) India
http://www.cyberwit.net
Tel: +(91) 9415091004
E-mail: info@cyberwit.net

Printed at Repro India Limited.

For Lora

Foreword

Everyone experiences or has been through their own personal exile: from themselves, from their families, from religion, from their countries and governments... These poems, (exiles in their own way), are a way of working out my vision and version of it, pondering and exploring ideas of exile. A dictionary definition might go like this: to banish a people, or an individual, as punishment, and force them out of their homeland. Exile means to suffer isolation, and implies approbation and loneliness. It often happens on the physical plane, which involves savage uprooting, excommunication, and a radical change of address.

The Jews were the original Biblical exiles: Moses, Exodus and the Promised Land etc. (It's interesting to note that the Ten Commandments are largely and widely ignored today). Out of exile, the Jews continued to have a torrid time throughout history. The annals also contain notorious exiles: Napoleon languishing on St. Helena, Lord Byron, Alexander Solzhenitsyn, Burgess and Maclean (British spies who defected to the cold), and Josef Brodsky, the exiled poet of St. Petersburg. There are many notable exemplars. The Nazarene himself was an exile, persecuted in the name of politics and faith, nailed to a cross. More fancifully, exile could involve the banishing of a medieval knight to dwell and rot forever in distant lands. Or more seriously, untold numbers of nameless political prisoners, disappeared in the Gulags of the world. We have witnessed whole nations being banished, amid sweeping sanctions in dismal, global confrontations. And Brexit has been and gone, a process of the UK's self-exile, reckless or otherwise, which has gone down as an historic and infamous act, a stab at Europe. The world has seen hordes of political exiles and refugees from one calamity or another over the centuries.

We can also consider more personal aspects of exile. Firstly, is the place of exile physical or mental? And secondly, has banishment taken place by force or by choice? I am, for example, writing this in a kind of exile of my own making: an Englishman in Moscow. Exile, in fact, is many things, from a lonely, hard-of-hearing old lady neglected in her flat, to the heroin addict existing in extremis, in exile from reality itself; lovers on different continents, painful separations, loyalties and families divided. There are many shades and variations of exile.

Sometimes, it seems that we are temperamentally exiled from the past itself, adrift, lost at sea in the sense that we can't really fully grasp it objectively. So we judge and sentence history and its important figures according to the current mores, unable to distinguish its actual soul and progressive, evolutionary nature. Mark Twain wrote: 'To arrive at a just estimate of a renowned man's character one must judge it by the standards of his time, not ours.' Another problem with history is that it frequently gets rewritten to suit the victors. Lies spread like wildfire while the truth freezes in Siberia! Napoleon Bonaparte noted the political tendency of reshaping, reworking, and misrepresenting history.

Another kind of exile is self-imposed by artists, sports people, dancers, writers, and musicians. Those engaged in the arts and professional sport are involved in processes demanding strict application. The loneliness of the long-distance runner… blood, sweat and tears… perspiration… the 10,000 hours… They are 24-hour obsessions that many are intimidated by because they take place in rarified and isolated spaces requiring much sacrifice and pain.

Some people feel like exiles in their own bodies, a physiological, psychological and philosophical conundrum leading to non-identification with assigned gender. Others just feel out of place, that somehow they don't belong. Perhaps they were born in the wrong country at the wrong time. They feel strange, a touch alien, and often have trouble relating to people. Then there are the restless souls, unable to settle, always on the move. Home is wherever I hang my hat. And how many suffer the exile of mental illness, and opt for extreme and suicidal solutions?

Exile is many things, and state of mind and perspective are important because it's not all bad. If you stay long enough, the place of your exile can become a refuge from the shrill noise of the world at large. While there are positives to be found everywhere and in anything (the bottle is always half full), it must be said that there is the threat of potential exile and marginalization these days, should you not think correctly. Freedom of speech has become the ball that got kicked into touch. The censors are out there with sharpened pencils ready to cross you out, and spike you. Red card. Disqualified. Game over. Exposing the crimes of the great and powerful, who dictate and own everything, has rarely been more out of fashion than it is today. And yet it has rarely been more necessary; it's a bad idea to exile truths and provide sanctuary for lies. That's how you install antichrists and exile history itself, how you bury it and render it bogus.

Protesting that lies are rampant and should be corrected is often a reason people get banished. Nevertheless, dissidents are necessary, they are the truth-seekers, rare in a mendacious world, and poetry must, as ever, stand for and exemplify Truth and Beauty. It must shine a light in the darkness, and celebrate the wonder and intrinsic unity of humanity and nature, in which, in reality, no exile, borders or boundaries exist.

Steve Elliott

Moscow

CONTENTS

BAPTISM

In a cold fold of Catholic gloom
and high stained windows,
in the incense-teeming air
the babe was duly anointed:
stinging water, pious shock.
Later, advisers and teachers.

Rituals, rites and rosaries.
A pocketful of poesies!
The ineluctability of an education.
Then banished, vanished across borders
along snaking lines of incantatory names,
learning a kind of forgetting along the way.

THE TRAVELLER

Bent I was on taking my leave.
So, I left, first heading north.
'There are things I must see,
exotic air I must breathe,'
I said before my setting forth.

North was a cold, desolate place;
I turned south for sun on my back,
and less wind and rain in my face.
I left a print, a spoor, some trace
on the long and lonesome track.

From South I turned about again,
beating a course to the East.
But there I found I was the same;
this caused me not a little pain—
I thought I'd be wiser, at least.

AUTOBIOGRAPHY

Inchoate wanderlust stirred,
waving from the nursery window,
beckoning beyond the billowing curtain.
A Steinway hammered from the next room,
and Mother's soprano soared above
Father's fingers arpeggiating—
Gretchen Am Spinnrade.
I clambered and grasped at the light,
escaping into the bigness of it all.
Later: London buses, vanguards of red,
the splintering neons of Piccadilly Circus,
the glittering sweep of Regent Street, and
Mother tripping gaily through Harvey Nicks.
Then maybe a Lion's Teahouse for a bite to eat,
before going on to a show or the flicks.
Strolling down the Strand
to a glittering spectacle in theatre land.
I sat in the pit watching him wave his stick;
that was *my* dad glaring at the clarinetist playing flat.
Later, we argued about Rock 'n' Roll and
Jimi Hendrix. He said it was a noise, and
'Why hear that when you could listen to Mozart?'
We travelled of course.
Father: 'We're going to Rio.'
He had a gig there: 'Lovely opera house!'
Mother was with *Lilac Time*
and sent postcards from Cape Town.
All the rage, electric on stage,
show time, perpetual transit…

Last call for Johannesburg!
Five minutes to curtain!
Darling, you look divine!
'It's all change,' Father said.
'We're going to Africa instead.'
Way down south,
under a blood-red moon,
I remember jacarandas in bloom,
and vivid pools on burnished lawns,
and apartheid: the elephant in the room.
We left him to face the music.
Some things are *verbied.*

We flew out of Joburg,
Mother, brother and I,
stopping in Nairobi and Rome,
returning to Shropshire's wintering hills:
exiles stumbling on stony ground,
no longer welcome in the hallowed halls
of the ancestral home.
So, I boarded a train of thought
and bought a ticket to Kathmandu.
I sat in a circle of saddhus, crouched,
barefoot by a burning ghat
on my journey to the East.

LORD VISHNU'S PEARL

Heading East, swerving out of the West,
hurtling through Balkan towns,
hammering down dark roads on a quest
to hurdle the horizons; sights and sounds
became another, something fresh and new,
as if music transposed to an unknown key
with wilder rhythms, unfenced and free.
In the diminishing miles a distance grew.

What had we so recently left behind?
High streets, pubs, football and beer;
9-to-5 weekdays and the daily grind—
7 am jolt to factory, office, dismal career…
Coughing, sneezing; ingurgitated news;
city folk in three-piece, pin-striped suits,
hair thinning and dyed at the roots.
Desperation spreading like a bruise!

Kaleidoscope of colour, pungent smells—
we had alighted on a disparate world
of patchouli, betel nut and temple bells;
all bedazzled by Lord Vishnu's pearl!
The people stared through curious eyes.
Where were we from, why had we come?
Mad English under India's burning sun…
To find ourselves! Whatever that implies.

JAIPUR 1979

I sat with my suntan,
and my shadow,
in a teashop in Jaipur,
exile at the edge of a decade.
Loosed from Western cradles,
and various fashion mistakes,
we ordered *chai* and *chillums*
and got high with saddhus,
ex-bankers and other criminals:
the girl from Dusseldorf
with the subversive mouth;
the scowling Sardinian
soured by Red Brigade encounters;
the heroin addict from Marseille,
pedalling moonstones for a fix;
an amorous Belgian getting screwed
for a fee by a London hedge;
hollow-eyed dope fiends;
orange-clad neophytes,
the *sannyasins* of Osho,
and even some genuine tourists
banging on about temples and bad toilets.
We had washed up
with our addictions and egos intact.
Itinerant and *poste restante*,
we had come to the holiest of places,
where the cows have right of way,
where dish and trident are venerated,
where even the dogs are more spiritual:

motley outlaws, decadent pilgrims,
anaesthetized, beaded, tie-dyed,
spiritually toe-dipped,
naked and blaspheming,
high on ragas, dip sticked,
destined to return, possibly,
to an address in Ealing,
an apartment in Rome,
a Paris district…
Home, where stuff worked and toilets flushed,
but where smiles and gestures were sterile
as warehouses full of coat hangers.
A neon world of fever and depression
broadcast 24/7.
So we had gone East,
but hadn't belonged there either:
fish out of water floundering in the heat
and dust, exotic targets easily speared.
We had to return to the spawning grounds,
the hustings, and the rat race of cold truths
and diminishing returns.
It was there in the runes.
Meanwhile, out in the Thar Desert,
in the rippling haze,
a camel train toiled across the sand.
I longed to join
the red-turbaned Rajasthani man,
(face like carved wood, grooved by wind and time),
and disappear beyond the dunes.

LOCKDOWN WITH UMBERTO ECO

In lockdown,
I read *Foucault's Pendulum.*
Hermetically sealed,
far from the clan,
in quarantine,
chronicling a saeculum.

An esoteric, arcane plan:
Templars in the Holy Land;
the madness of windmills;
mapless questing through Judaean hills;
beating about a burning bush,
exiled in a bowl of dust.

JOHANNESBURG 1968

Can you remember
the fiery plumes and vivid blooms
of those southern gardens,
aquamarine pools shimmering
on water-thirsting lawns?

Can you remember
the gold mines and limousines,
the stink of money,
and the jacaranda-lined drive
where we'd sit at five?

Can you remember
our guilt over the filth
and suffering in sad Soweto,
reeling away, not speaking,
retreating from the unspeakable?

Can you remember
the scarred faces, native fear,
the corrosive hatred:
the Bantu trampled
under a fascist boot?

DEATH OF AN ADDICT

1

It's known that Graham Greene
liked a bit of opium and being unseen:
from Argentina to Vietnam,
on the lam, off the beaten track…

My tale starts in West Ham,
where my friend read his novels:
Stamboul Train and all that.
He burned with wanderlust
and chased the dragon of dreams,
on a journey to Kathmandu or bust.

Spaced out in eastern hovels
in a mud sprawl of ramshackle huts;
that's where he read *Brighton Rock,*
while vicious amoebas slashed his guts,
and he got sicker than a dog.

But there was no nursie
to ease the pain,
so morphine became
his sister of mercy.

He roamed the sub-continent
from Kulu to Cochin,
staying in temples

when the money ran thin,
like the pain-wracked flesh
falling from his body,
desiccated by the opium poppy.

2

Bag of bones,
lying in grime,
rags for clothes…
He left behind:
a notebook of poems;
a ticket for a ferry;
a copy of *The Quiet American*,
and a hypodermic.
Nothing much besides.

It turned out he could not be saved;
perhaps oblivion is what he craved.

This is what he wrote the day he died
in cheap lodgings in Old Delhi;
last entry before the final exit,
disease lodged deep in his belly:

3

'I like to feel the spike
puncture my skin
before the smack rushes in
and blots everything
out!

Then I am Shiva
in the eye of a needle;
my lips go blue,
retching on the floor
in the dust and the poo.

Yet it looks like a palace
containing wonders:
the rusted nail in the wall
piercing the tit of a pin-up—
my Caravaggio.

The chipped, brown mug,
a magnificent chalice
where some alchemist
has transmuted tea leaves
into flecks of gold.

In my pools of vomit
there are rubies
and emeralds and stars.
I swan dive backwards,
collapse in the arms of

my dame, my mistress,
in bliss and forgetfulness.
And I don't give a damn
about any of all this,
and I'm dying to die again!'

JESUS STREET

I like to go down in the dirt
where desolation fumes;
that's where Jesus does his work,
not in genteel rooms.

I go down where lepers rot,
and bathe and kiss their feet;
the least of them are my flock,
I don't live on *Easy Street.*

I cannot worship gain and loss,
nor demons sprouting horns.
So you can nail me to a cross
and crown my head with thorns.

A MEMORY OF TROUT

Have I moved on
any further after the wrench
of upping sticks
and coming to a place like this?

Cold panorama,
bleak block, paradox
of a singular red sock.

… memories:
weeping willows
shading seven stepping stones,
where rainbow trout
rose in a river
winding passed
lobelia and hollyhock.

All so long ago!
Though, I see them still:
darts in the flow;
electric, elusive,
pure quicksilver.

ORDYNKA

When you live, half exiled
from your own native lingo,
sunk by Slavic syllables, adrift
so to speak, in floundering talk,

it's like navigating foreign parts
without a map or compass.
And all the signs are in Cyrillic,
leading to an impasse.

Voices reverberate as if in a well.
Gurgling from a Soviet tank.
Rumour near Patriarch Ponds.
Bulgakov on the brain.

And it's a headache to explain
to the *babushka* down the hall
that the bog's on the blink.
Again! I've gone blank!

Try to describe the scene.
How to formulate it as such?
I blurt out the price of grapefruit;
I'm learning to say, 'How much?'

But I am powerless it seems
to grasp such a demotic tongue;
she could be selling talcum powder,
or planning to plant a bomb.

We're lost up Translation Alley,
somewhere near Ordynka.
Send a code breaker, please!
And something for this stinker.

BRITS

Boldly go the bald men.
Exit Great Britain!
Union Jack shorts
and beer bellies
bulged in elasticated strain.

A hooligan mentality:
the football scores
and dodging the Old Bill,
fish 'n' chips and English ale,
culture fail, roadkill, fatality.

Shrill wives of course,
foul-mouthed grannies
and a blue murder of brats.
Tattooed arses
and ludicrous hats,

planted on Benidorm
and places like that.
Any port in a storm—
Watch out! The Brits are coming
to piss on your lawn.

BILL OF RIGHTS

The past is weighed to judge its lessons.
Progressio in futuras, we dish out the blame,
and some contend that what we did
all those years ago was a crying shame.
Are these peculiarly modern obsessions?
Should we grasp and lift the grimy lid,
claiming we shouldn't have said this or that
about any old sex, or white or black,
about the dog days and dark nights,
that we should rewrite the Bill of Rights?
You may ask where all this might end.
We used to enjoy freedom of speech.
Is it something you can bend out of reach
simply by having a big enough spend?

STUFF THE APOCALYPSE!

These days I stare through windows
at friendly leaves waving from trees.
I spend hours contemplating motes
of sunlight percolating on parquet.
I magnify tiny worlds through a lens,
to grasp perhaps a bigger picture,
and some few harmonious notes.

Anything to stall the flights of hysteria,
the *Whitehall Farce* of an idiotic world
dropping its trousers and shitting bricks.
It isn't real, so stuff your apocalypse!

Let me peel the headlines from my eyelids
and fling them in the garbage,
or recycle them into wings of doves.

SIBERIA

You're no good,
your blood's no good,
your forecast's doomed.

Your ears flap in the snow,
they're no good,
your hearing's bad.

We don't want your books
And your lofty poets
can get stuffed!

They're no good!
Your great composers
can piss right off.

Your money's no good,
it's frozen solid,
you're in the red.

Good for nothing,
you're exiled,
you'll stay in Siberia.

BURGESS & MACLEAN

Burgess went to Moscow
& Maclean too
those British spies
ditched in Red Square:
two birds of a feather
flapping in the icy weather.

Burgess & Maclean
were politically unclean:
the sparrow and the hawk:
one upper-crust, alcoholic,
outcast, banished,
return-tickets? *Nyet, nix!*

The other integrated:
Burgess learned the lingo,
made his English useful
and was happy it seemed.
But both defected
because they had a dream.

MEGALOMANIA

Napoleon broods on Helena:
'I call foul—
the victors get to
write my history now!'
C'est pas possible!
C'est misérable!
C'est terrible!
C'est exécrable
Bonaparte broods
upon the ruins of empire,
and how he was
cruelly exiled.
He bemoans
the lost campaign,
his Waterloo —
the megalomania.

IN THE COLD

This is where hell freezes,
where men get pulped
to grotesque parodies
and coffin-eyed shadows:
Labour Camp, Vorkuta,
Northern Siberia.
Knifing winds blow ill:
minus 34, rags for boots,
wrong clothes and perishing,
thin *Gulag* rations;
potato bits in boiled water,
nothing nourishing.
The weak are doomed.
There are many dead.
The strong survive. Just.
Chewing wallpaper and leather!
But the muse's drive
against Arctic chill
and slaving 10 hours a day
keeps the poet alive:
the story must be told.
Just keep going, find scraps,
anything to write on,
and something to write with.
Take your pen, it's like gold,
and write poetry in the cold.

SUICIDE MISSION

I have been caressed by razors,
cut open by careless knives,
dissected on frigid slabs
under the glint of wanton eyes;
chopped indiscriminately by axes,
sliced by sharp remarks.

I have exchanged bodily fluids
with beggars and whores.
My bones became relics
strewn around the Holy Church.
Millennia spinning on a skewed axis.
Where lies multiplied, Truth died!

I have been nailed to crosses
from Calvary to Kansas,
my tongue cut out by a cruel king
for speaking out of turn;
inquisitors put me on the rack
and the screws turned.

I was hauled over burning coals
in the dungeons of dark overlords,
and called *traitor, blasphemer*!
I was broken on rolling presses;
my words lost in the wind,
drowned by lunatics shrilling.

A machine with no soul
cast me into a desert of ashes
in a fallout of bitter lies;
I was drawn into the vortex
of a thousand skirmishes—
the mission was always suicide.

BRODSKY

1
Akhmatova thrilled at its Moorish design.
Alexander Blok had rooms in the enfilade.
The building was the talk of St. Petersburg,
that aqueous city of canals and bridges,
hotbed of revolution and historic crime.
Outside, the street describes a rolling curve
around cupolas and Orthodox awnings,
then sweeps on to the Fontana River
and into the Summer Gardens' shade,
where Pushkin strolled on sunlit mornings.

2
I am nearby, standing *in a room and a half,*
here in this high-ceilinged Soviet garret:
Joseph Brodsky's place, 24 Liteiny Prospect,
looking out on three streets and a square.
Today, it's a museum, so I'm a paying guest.
I pace around, brooding in Brodsky's place,
noting our continents of exile are reversed.
I imagine Joseph building his barricade;
those cannily contrived constructions
are walls to keep his parents at bay.

3
Two ceiling-high arches were problematic:
no room for privacy, however provisional
in his 33% of the one and a half rooms.
The partition doesn't have to be discreet,

just incomplete, so as to avoid suspicion
and tittle-tattle to the building commission.
Brodsky blocks his parents out with precarious
piles of books and suitcases to the ceiling.
They suppose that it can't really do any harm,
and grudgingly accept Joseph's new *Lebensraum*.

4
Maria Brodsky scrubs all to a Christian shine,
polishes the parquet and dusts the lampshade
above the table where spotless linen lies.
She sits at the *Singer,* her thrifty hands fly,
mending shirt collars, trousers and flies.
In her lap, no bourgeois luxury, just scraps;
nothing is wasted when you're scratching by.
Alexander has been tinkering with his camera
and announces *Swan Lake* will start in five;
they watch it on a 1952 Soviet television set.

5
Mr. Brodsky is a naval man, a commander,
landlubbered by the Navy for being Jewish.
Threats were aired, they'd been prepared to flee
the dictator's decree of exile and transportation.
But then Stalin died in '53, so that was that.
The Russian Navy had years of Alexander,
in a world war from Romania's seas to China's.
Like all Russians, and some 27 million fell,
Alexander did his bit and tried to do it well,
for war was too close to home in Leningrad.

6

His dark naval coat was like a night street;
the double rows of glowing golden buttons
shone like lamps lit along an avenue.
Father guide, he revealed the city to his son,
from the *Winter Palace* to the *Field of Mars*,
over the bridges and through watery byways.
At the city's Navy Museum, he was captain
among astrolabes, sextants, and binnacles,
and portraits of clean-shaven admirals;
salt water always was Alexander's element.

7

Indelible are memories of Leningrad's siege;
only the strong survived its death-dealing
hardships at minus forty-two degrees;
starvation began in the winter of forty-one,
cruel after the thirties' murderous activity.
Born free before Revolution, before captivity,
and they are Jews, the Brodsky's, to boot.
But Alexander and Maria just get on with it,
stoical under the steel heel of the system,
and with Joseph, their wayward son,

8

now day-dreaming up the 14-foot walls
into a blue-green tracery of archipelagos.
Two 10-foot chests rise up, cliffs of oak with
capacious depths rivalling basements or attics,
containing the Brodsky's bounty and artefacts:
Father's cameras, Mother's scarves and hats,
tablecloths, china, dishes, shoes and linen,

faded supplements, family albums, bric-à-brac,
tools, batteries, binoculars, broken torches,
her garish kimonos, fans, and other mementoes.

9
Yet by far the household's greatest object,
a marvel much prized, envied, and coveted,
is the conjugal bed of royal proportions:
a vast Art Nouveau, Constructivist ark
in light brown maple that never creaks.
Island, oasis, sickbay, haven in the dark,
where, along with the sheets, life is aired.
The command vessel is an inviolable fixture,
anchored and harboured in the family's bosom.
And Joseph's existence got started there.

10
These 1.5 rooms are in a *kommunalka*;
communal living in Soviet style dictates
nine square metres for each Ivan and Irina.
The kitchen, bathroom and bog are shared,
and Joseph knows who's sitting in there
by the sound and smell of the residents' farts.
In the kitchen, the women gather and gossip,
comparing the tribulations of their days.
This is where it all ends, or starts;
this is your life sentence, yes, for always!

11
You will never move from this place;
rising above what you are is impossible;
your lot is to graft for the common good.
Comrade, you're both prisoner and warden,

informer on sinful and un-Soviet thoughts.
You must sacrifice any ambitious notions,
and obey the State's laws and all its motions.
Living cursed, under the strictest of terms,
Joseph Brodsky is heading for a fall.
After all, he's a poet and they always burn.

12
This is where the troublemaking loafer lies,
slave-bound by Soviet and family ties.
Voracious reader, broadening his horizons
beyond ideologically permitted boundaries.
Was Brodsky born too soon or too late,
after culture's tree was felled by the State
and Lenin baldly presented his *fait accompli*?
Wings clipped, by ruthless talons restrained!
His poor parents hardly deserved their fate:
to be born free but to live and die in chains.

13
And what shall become of the wayward son?
Akhmatova's prodigal poet will be branded
pornographic, anti-Soviet. He will be reviled
for a weak *paranoid reformist delusion*,
and be committed to a mental institution.
Banished to the north for *social parasitism*,
he is generally deemed a worthless citizen.
Finally, they send Joseph Brodsky into exile,
via Austria, never to return to Russian soil,
leaving his parents eternally stranded.

14
Auden finds him sanctuary in the US of A,
where he's lionized and wins the Nobel Prize.

Brodsky compares the complacent freedoms
of this new exile to the fetters he left behind.
And a great farce drags on for over a decade:
his parents' applications to visit are denied:
twelve years of languishing in chancelleries
before implacable counters where hopes fade.
He's resigned never to see them again,
and it's useless to resist or complain.

15
When Maria goes, the first crow appears
in the pines behind his place in South Hadley.
Thirteen months later, Alexander croaks in his chair,
and a second crow flaps in like an omen.
Brodsky ponders the final exile, which is death,
and wonders how his parents really felt
in that winnowing away before the final breath.
No more calls, no undelivered letters now
to Liteiny Prospekt, Number 24, Flat 28,
which is currently someone else's address.

16
And so we die, each in our own exile,
each with feelings that leave us bereft.
But it's nothing to do with the geography of it;
such dilemmas always end in separations,
in a seething gulf that brooks no defences.
Yet Brodsky feels no real remorse or grief.
He remains Russian amid the white picket fences.
Perhaps, he reasons, it's some kind of relief
from loneliness and endless visa applications,
and the *one and a half rooms* he left.

* Brodsky was inspired by Joseph Brodsky's autobiographical In a Room and a Half, written in English in America around 1984/5, some dozen years after his exile from the USSR, and just before he won the Nobel Prize for Literature in 1987. The great English poet W. H. Auden helped Brodsky get to the US. In a Room and a Half recalls Brodsky's childhood in Leningrad (now St. Petersburg) in the communal Soviet flat, where he grew up and lived with his parents. Brodsky's old place is now a museum.

LORD BYRON

Canting over cantos, Byron's in decline.
Tumultuous, wanton, sacrilegious,
he quaffs from a skull rare claret wine.
It's said he kept a bear at college.
Lord Byron: 'Mad, bad and dangerous
to know!' — as is common knowledge.
Exiled, the roving poet repairs to Rome.
Disowned by his race, a deformed freak,
he perishes, in 1824, far from home,
fighting for independence for the Greek.

EXILE IN AN EASY CHAIR

Mrs. E: exiled in an easy chair,
in a council flat in West Ham.
Deafness isolates.
And there's the loneliness too.
That's why the telly's blaring—
fifteen hours a day!
(But the smack addicts
next door don't give a damn).
No one visits.
The kids are grown up
and live far away.
It's bloody miles and miles!
She tuts at the news,
brews a pot during ad breaks,
swoons at old movies,
falls in love with the glitzy smiles
of game show hosts.
She seems happy enough,
with her knitting and her fags,
sitting among the rags of her life.

ROLLING STONES

At least they didn't go
and do what Lennon did:
say they were more popular than Jesus!
For Christ's sake, John!
Nevertheless: trashed, harassed,
pinned like butterflies,
dirty, greasy, stigmatized:
You wouldn't want your daughter or sister
going out with one of them, would you?
...created quite a name for *disturbance*,
but it was good publicity
railing against the establishment
with a *street-fighting man;*
all that flailing and jumping about.
Jack Flash jiving to the *Satisfaction*
of young people rocking the boat.
After all, *it was a gas, gas, gas...*
to be in revolt.
The sixties were a trip,
time for getting your *rocks off*,
advocating peace and love,
and smoking funny cigarettes.
You got the silver, you got the gold...
another million sold.
Just another mad, mad day on the road.
And through suicides and homicides,
and war being *just a shot away,*
into raucous exile the show rolled on
to palm trees and Mediterranean skies,

and snare-drum punctuated nights,
the voodoo, the boogie, Jagger's dance,
far out, and far from *Main Street,*
with the stars looking down
at the stars on the ground,
tax-exiled and glimmering
in the South of France.

CYNTHIA

Swift clouds ply peculiar boats above
her: white sails gliding across the face
of the moon, full and beaming its love,
inspiring the unbridled tide to race
up the shore and hiss over the sand.
She closes it all in the palm of her hand,
a pearl to glisten deep within a pocket.
She cannot speak of Cynthia, long dead,
held close to heart in a golden locket;
there are many things she leaves unsaid,
but a note is written so they may trace
the dark side cratered inside her head;
she will not be released from this lunacy,
and wades out to sink in a moonlit sea.

LONG DISTANCE LOVE

Hark! the voice starts,
as if breaking into
a song unto itself:

voices diverse as snowflakes,
rising and falling,
are whispering and talking now:

an utterance from Beijing;
Moscow is calling;
gossip from West Malling.

The multitudes sing.
There is a sighing in your ear
and the telephone rings:

a girl in Tokyo speaks.

SYLVIA

A fathomless rage
flares from the page.
Storms on the moon,
claw tearing at cage.

Take a spoon
and null the pain.
Diamond tongue,
how delicately done,

wrought and finely spun.
Filigree sun,
catcher of rain.
Pearls of wisdom each one.

The oyster clings to its jewel,
clutched in silent depths,
clamped and tenacious,
jealous as Poseidon!

Sylvia stirs the sea
into a cataclysm of grief,
and extinguishes the stars,
one by one.

EXTREME GAS

One fine day,
in her flat,
she stuck her head in the oven.

Rumours? A dime a dozen!
What drove her to that
extremity of the soul?

Despair? Lack of air?
Nazis in the closet?
What was it?

How did the husband react?
Any debate?
Anything to retract?

The coroner wrote: 'Suicide'.
At any rate,
the poet died.

FREE BIRDS

How cheerful are the free birds
here at my prison bars, quite a throng!
Quartets of chirping sound,
my sadness lost, happiness found.
They sing their souls' song,
which is too beautiful for words.

RED OCTOBER

October! How the spendthrift trees
squander their legions of leaves:
tumbling notes of copper and gold.
Spring and summer's hot routine
kept the balance crisp and green.

But red October ushers in the cold
and winter rehearses in the wings.
About the house, a shrill wind sings
from skies as miserable as Mondays.
The chill-eyed banker appears on cue,
demanding what is clearly overdue:
a golden raiment strewn at his feet;
more leaves than you could sweep
in a month of gruelling Sundays.

SWAN

For Galina Samsova
Perfected synthesis of body and mind.
What is she if not poetry in motion?
Sinew and muscle that fluidly find
precisely the poise, rhythm and flow
of a choreographed intricate design.
She's lifted high on a crest of emotion
that carries its force beyond the stage,
rolling over the audience like a wave.
Breathless, we witness the dying fall,
then the flourish, and the final bow;
argosies of bouquets are presented now.
She's like her flowers, fragile and small.
Grace and beauty! A rapturous refrain.
But are those tears of happiness, or of pain?

MILERS

For Steve Ovett

Lean of limb, milers are a special breed:
four even quarters 'gainst clock and man;
rare combination of endurance and speed;
strong opponents, and the ticking hand;
four laps in under a four-minute span.
The gun propels the mile into its stride,
the pace is brisk and the runners glide.
The first lap unwinds, early in the game,
while the second passes with little strain.
Spiked shoes dig into the blood-red track;
the third lap's an exile of mounting pain,
steeling mind and body for the final attack.
The bell clangs: last quarter to the tape
and the winning kick in the home straight.

CLIMATE CHANGE

A lake once lapped a lush green shore
before an eternity of dust appeared:
parched, cracked, desolate ground,
idols slouching in the lost and found.
Eons and eons more. Locusts in hordes.
In the God forge, humanity is cleared.
How much time does time compound?
Ages elapsed before fields of wheat
rustled again, thriving in rain and heat.
Rise and fall, relapse and collapse.
And how many exiled peoples fled,
or were put to merciless swords,
crushed and ground to destruction?
Death knell and final corruption.

A quite thrilling and diverting game!

Another go! We're under starter's orders.
But Armageddon's alarming all the same.
Rien ne va plus, bet on the human race,
embrace all kindness, love and grace.
Encore, Zeitgeist, and some civilised talk,
winding along the herbaceous borders.
And don't forget to use the right fork!
Mr. Eliot and Dante argue in the pantry.
Folk 'round here just *come and go...*
while the croupier spins another throw.
Nobody needs a Doctor of Divinity,
Bob Dylan, or even the Holy Trinity
to know which way the Horsemen churn:
tides turn, Rome fiddles, emperors burn.

THE FOG

I met Tommy on the pier at Southend:
days of *Rock against Racism... Dr. Feelgood...*
White Boy on a diet, light as a petal,
too sharp and too thin for heavy metal.
The frantic jive, the patois, the babble,
scoring meth from a hood in the back.
In those days, it was the high of fashion.
He called me *Mein Liebling,* his Sistine Chapel.
He mounted my pulpit with all his passion,
our heads floating not far from the ceiling.
Gabbling on, (you know how it gets),
about Jazz and the holy spirit of Stan Getz:
myriad connections and crossed wires,
profanities, vanities, and bonfires.

Tonight he's lit up again, mind streaming;
there is so much, so many things to say,
insights all gilded with iconic revelation.
Tommy speaks of a visit from Kerouac's ghost,
then *Pearl & Dean* projected in dreams,
and how to spread butter on hot toast:
generously, thick, and even, it seems.
Memory slips to his forty-fifth birthday,
when we danced all night with Beaujolais,
spliffs and poetry, which is Tommy's religion.
Then he loses it: another kick in the psyche!
He insists there is no theological solution,
although there may be provisional salvation.
Then he rants on about poverty and deprivation:

Somewhere on a hill of filth, wraiths
scratch like dogs through turds and tips!

Tommy goes silent and mutters at the wall.
What to do? Well, he does love his trips.
What about taking a southbound train, stall
the gloom, and put a smile on his lips?
Storm the old pier, jukebox switch in hand,
then leapfrog like lunatics across the sand.
Ah! Wouldn't that be utter blissfulness?
But we're crashing now like the breakers.
Eyes telegraphing a bleary wistfulness,
Tommy begins to fumble for his works,
to drift oblivious on a pillow of poppies.
And over the drear, dilapidated acres,
and the two-up-two-down terraced sprawl,
a fog begins to fall.

VOX HUMANA

Imagine a voice.
Disembodied.
Exiled.
A lone cry.
A conscience, a chorus:
Beware the ides of March!

Vox nullius generis,
no nation, no nothing,
no creed, no politics,
no ideology as such.
Just a voice keening
in the ruins and the dust.

And the voice asks:
Why do you love to hate?
It is neither
your natural condition,
nor your purpose
in this universe.

PROMISED LAND

History habitually makes a mess:
things go awry
from Calvary to Capitol Hill.
The spirit of Dreyfus
moaned from Devil's Island.
Omens went unheeded,
the wind was ill:
Auschwitz, Buchenwald…
the spectre of *Eichmann…*
in for the kill…
2,000 years of Christendom
cannot reconcile the divide
that haunts us still today:
exiles are often heard to say:
Why is that promised land
never near enough at hand?

SON OF MAN

Prodigious plagues
in the Pharaoh's land:
water turned to blood;
pestilence of locusts;
frog-clotted mud.

Wind and sands;
incarnadine seas;
famine and disease;
worshipping Baal—
sacrificing the children.

God commanded otherwise;
his anger burned in a bush.
Moses, subsumed in ashes,
brought down the tablets
from Jehovah's mountain.

The Messiah finally arrives—
marvellous miracle-maker
from loaves and fishes.
But politically unsound,
his Way is stony ground:

Pilate washes his hands,
condemning the Son of Man
to drag cruciform
and crown-of-thorn—
adorned upon a Roman nail!

The light gutters on Golgotha;
crucified under angry Judean skies,
with the women crying,
and the soldiers sweating
and cursing the length of his dying.

BORDER CLOSED

This land is strangled in red tape:
rubber stamps proliferate like weeds;
bureaucrats muzzle poetry's mouth;
censors commit intellectual rape.

Have your papers with you at all times,
otherwise there'll be hell to pay—
beaten till you're black and blue
and levied with heavy fines.

Your documents are not in order.
Fill in this form, stand in that line.
You must wait your turn to be rejected.
And note: you're exiled at the border.

East & West

The rift between East and West—
how should it best be righted?
If the ethereal and material were united,
humans would be blessed.

Out of the Western world
came a machine-driven reality;
from the East sprang spirituality,
and wisdom's pearl.

If ever the twain should meet,
heaven would be within reach;
this is what the mahatmas preach,
but disunity is our defeat.

25 DECEMBER

And so this is *not* Christmas in the land
that once tried to abolish Christianity.
All good comrades asserted the anathema
of the bourgeois kid from Bethlehem.
But priests still lurked in the villages:
black-cassocked, bearded and brazen,
clutching slanted Orthodox crosses.
The *babushkas* hoarded their icons,
kept in that special place
reserved for numerous and various saints,
cowering in the corner with Yeshua.

Party poopers put Christmas in a steel box
and left it to rot for seven decades.
They turned the churches into warehouses
for lumber and less-than-divine paraphernalia;
secular myopia excluded all smacking of religion.
But, in time, Communism's dark cathedrals
tumbled and crumbled in the restructured dust,
crushed under the weight of ungodly pageants.
Resurrected: 70 years' exile in the *Gulags,*
walled up by implacable slogans,
Christ rose out of the detritus and chaos.

And yet this is still *not* Christmas!
For most it is merely an after-thought,
falling in the bleak grey days of January,
when all you want to do is stay drunk indoors.
Cold winds shriek down winter-wide avenues.

Its spirit is frozen solid: ghost, paradox
in the land of a billion Christmas trees.
Yuletide will not be redeemed;
there will be no thaw, no ho-ho-ho,
although Christ will rise again at Easter,
and be proclaimed as risen.

LETTER FROM EXILE

How to describe Siberia?
You can say it's big,
and there *are* a lot of trees!
Snow in winter, devilish cold,
brief hot flaring summers.
Berry-picking days

and idling in the forest.
Long evenings of solitude.
Time enough to write sagas!
And to read and mark
all the works of man.
Time for contemplation.

How is Nevsky Prospekt,
the boats, canals, and White Nights?
Oh, the gaiety of St. Petersburg,
with its scheming underbelly.
A regime's reckless critic,
I burned all my bridges.

Painful is the memory of Papa
turning his face to the wall,
mute and dreadful as a bust.
And the old clock in the hall
striking my time for leaving,
warders and manacles waiting.

Well, you'll escape the city soon
for the dacha near Gatshina.
Give my love to each and all.
I am thinking of Papa now.
Sad he was never reconciled
to his son's happy exile:

felicitously gathering berries,
(dew-drenched rubies in the grass)
under canopies of Siberian fir.
I labour on most gladly,
repairing the steel rails
that never take me anywhere.

The express carries my letters
to cities distant as dreams now.
I accept it like an exegesis.
Thawed by my 15th spring,
it's hard to feel banishment
in a land as pure as this.

www.ingramcontent.com/pod-product-compliance
Ingram Content Group UK Ltd.
Pitfield, Milton Keynes, MK11 3LW, UK
UKHW041316190726
13845UKWH00025B/309

9 789363 546547